IMMANUEL

Poems and Meditations

on

The Life of Jesus

Thomas Ryder Worth

Audio version of this publication is also available on iTunes, Amazon, & Audible.

Book design by www.greatwriting.org
www.immanuelpoems.org

St. Paul, Looking unto Jesus: A detail from a painting by the author's brother, William Worth
(See further on page 76)

Words of Appreciation

"I want to thank you for the beautiful book you sent at Christmas on The Incarnation. My fiancé, Wayne, and I read the book together." —*PP*

"What a blessing and surprise it was to receive the unexpected gift of Thomas R. Worth's book *The Incarnation*! His poetry chosen for Advent is not only beautiful and inspiring for the Christmas season, but perfect for meditation all year long. Ms. Petsova's artwork is so lovely and helps to make this dear little book one to treasure for years." —*BC*

"Thank you so much for sending me the book *The Incarnation* by Thomas R. Worth. It has touched me deeply. I saw God in an entirely different light. His birth unto our world became so real! This book made him more real to me than any other spiritual experience in my 89 years, especially now that I am closer to seeing him face to face." —*MM*

"Thank you so much for the beautiful gift book *The Incarnation*. It is touching my heart with much thankfulness for our dear Savior." —*MC*

"Truly I have never received a thank you gift that has been such a continuing blessing to me. Each day my daughter and I—she lives away from me—talk on the phone and I read her and me that day's poem…. We spend lots of time thanking our Lord for these two blessings." —*MT*

"I have so enjoyed reading these poems, and I am only on the December 5th poem. I love pondering God's visuals to us: his creation like the moon, a picture of us receiving light from the son to a lost and dying world. Thank you again for this wonderful gift." —*SG*

"You've so entirely and eternally blessed me with your precious book/art work by Thomas Ryder Worth *The Incarnation*! So many reminders in it, for me to keep pressing forward!" —*JE*

"Immanuel offers us, in poetic form, a message that is so vital to the world. God has gifted men and women with the talent of expressing ideas in poetry. That gift, which I have often envied, is evident in this book. I believe this work is inspired of God and will be a blessing to thousands of people around the world. I encourage you to read it carefully—you will be both encouraged and challenged by its message. Thank you for this work of art that is a blessing and challenge to us all."
—John Bueno, Founder of ChildHope Ministries

"Every believer has his or her way of conveying biblical stories. Poetry is one such way that may take a little extra concentration; however, it's well worth the effort. The aim of the author 'to help people see Jesus in fresh ways' was definitely accomplished for me. Once I started to read a couple of the poems, I was drawn to read the rest. 'Listen to the Shepherds' was one of my favorites. The poems taken collectively contain an avalanche of gems that will enhance your understanding of the meaning of Immanuel 'God with us.'"
—Roger Jonker, Co-founder and Director of Father's Love Ministry

About World Challenge

World Challenge, Inc. was created by David Wilkerson in 1971 to expand the work of Teen Challenge and spread the gospel globally. Now his son, Gary Wilkerson, continues building this outreach, believing in the great power of God's Word to heal the sick and liberate the poor.

World Challenge is currently working in over forty countries, offering Bible training through pastors' conferences, relief care to widows and orphans, and continuing education to those caught in the cycle of poverty. The aim of these biblically based programs is to give people the practical tools to thrive mentally, physically, socially, financially, and spiritually. A transformed individual should be discipled in God's Word and trained to help transform their community.

Another branch of our work is dedicated to encouraging and building up those whose invaluable support allows us to continue our ministry. We create podcasts, articles, and videos to make Biblical resources easily accessible for everyone.

We firmly believe that the Holy Spirit, Biblical doctrine, and education can empower anyone to live a better life and make a better world.

Foreword by Gary Wilkerson

Our loving, compassionate God looks to bless us with his amazing favor. Nowhere is that more evident than in the miracle of Jesus' birth, life and ultimate sacrifice.

We may think God is only interested in our spiritual lives and not in our minds, bodies or emotions. Nothing could be further from the truth. No one can understand the day-to-day struggle better than Jesus who worked a hard, physical job and helped take care of his family for many years. Our incarnate Lord is intimately aware of life's highs and lows.

Christmas is a season of great celebration and joy, but it can also be a time of heavy fatigue, family drama and remembered sorrow.

If this is a hard season for you, don't despair. We have a good, good Father who is faithful to all of his children. He sent his Son to deliver us spiritually, mentally, emotionally and physically. God has given us so many beautiful promises of redemption and healing. This book will hopefully be a great reminder of what Jesus has done and is continuing to do for his redeemed, for you.

As one of the saints, you are called. You are chosen. You are part of a family that's impacting the world in ways that can never fully be measured.

This season, please remember how dearly you are loved.

With you in Christ,

Gary Wilkerson
PRESIDENT: World Challenge

The Risen Christ by the Sea of Tiberias

Acknowledgments

Marsha, my wife, has been my most ardent encourager and truest critic. For any poem to see the light of day, it had to pass her muster first. And you may rest assured, that the world has been saved at times from my attempts which did not meet her standard. She also helped me remember some early efforts which were worth including in this collection. Thanks to Jim Palumbo for putting pressure on me to publish a second collection. Thank you, Lord, for giving me a calling where my studies and meditations led to the creation of these poems. To the folks at World Challenge, I'm grateful to them for continuing to partner with me on these works, and to friends and neighbors at Community Covenant Church who have heard these poems as part of my sermons over the years; to Petrana Petsova for granting permission to publish some of her paintings to illustrate this collection and Nikolay Markov for facilitating her contribution; and to Jim Holmes, for putting it all together. Many thanks to all!

*

EDITOR'S NOTE: The spelling of Christ's name "God with us" as Immanuel is based on the romanization of the word from Hebrew, while Emmanuel is a translation of the Greek spelling. Both are used in original Biblical texts, and they have the same meaning. Neither is, strictly speaking, the correct spelling. For the purposes of this book, though, we have chosen to go with Immanuel since this is the word used in the Hebrew text of Isaiah 7:14.

A Note about the Poet and His Work

Tom Worth has been a pastor and Bible teacher in Evangelical circles since the early eighties. For over twenty-five years he has made annual mission trips to Bulgaria where he teaches in Evangelical churches. He and his wife, Marsha, have been married since 1974. They have two daughters who are married and who have supplied them with five precious grandchildren. He is a graduate of Pinecrest Bible Training Center and of SUNY Empire State College. He holds the M. Div. and the D. Min. from Northeastern Seminary in Rochester, NY. He is currently the pastor of Community Covenant Church in Manlius, NY, adjacent to Syracuse. He has served on the adjunct faculty of Pinecrest/Bethany and Northeastern Seminary. Tom Worth has a poetic-narrative way of teaching and preaching from the Scriptures where he seeks to help people see Jesus in fresh ways.

Preface

This collection of my poetry is inspired by the life of Jesus. My first collection was concerned mainly with Jesus' Incarnation and its implications. This collection draws not only from the Incarnation, but also from Jesus' life and ministry, as well as his death and resurrection. It also ventures occasionally into the Old Testament and draws from such stories as those of Noah, Jacob and Moses. It closes with a figure who got to know Jesus in somewhat the same way we do, after Jesus' Ascension. I mean, of course, Paul the Apostle.

In these poems I am pondering the mystery of our Lord Jesus as Immanuel, God with us. That is why those who encouraged me to publish this collection chose this title, Immanuel. These attempts to come to grips with the life of Jesus represent over four decades of wrestling with this mystery.

As I did last time, I encourage you to take your time through these poems. But I won't be as strict with my recommendations as I was then. Feel free to tackle as many as you want at a sitting. You may dip into it here and there, reading it that way if you like. Or you may read them in order, since it does follow a progression, beginning in the Old Testament, and then spending the bulk of the content with the story of Jesus, and ending with Paul setting an example for us to look to Jesus. As you read this book, may God bless you and help you to consider afresh Christ Jesus, who came and dwelt among us.

T. R. W., Syracuse, New York

A Note about the Artists

Tom Worth got to know Petrana Petsova over the course of his many mission trips to Silistra, Bulgaria. Petrana graduated from the School of Fine Arts in Sofia in 1979, while the country was deep in the grip of Communism. Even though she was forbidden to paint Christian or Biblical subjects, she persevered and endured harassment and persecution. At times the authorities confiscated and destroyed her paintings, but many have survived that menace. One such painting is her first effort at a Biblical painting. It is of Jesus serving breakfast to his disciples on the shores of the Sea of Galilee after his resurrection. This painting is on page 8. Since the fall of communism in 1989, Petrana has been quite prolific, painting hundreds of Biblical and historical subjects. Her home in Silistra, Bulgaria has become a picture gallery where her paintings line the walls and even the ceiling. The story is told that she had to hide her Christian-themed artwork in beehives from Communist authorities and so prevent them from being seized! She is quite elderly but vigorous, and she still paints for the glory of God and the love of the subject.

About William Worth, the Artist for the Front Piece and the End Piece
Tom Worth's brother, Bill, has been an artist all his life. Sketching and drawing come naturally to him. He is a graduate of Pinecrest Bible Training Center, the Portfolio Center in Atlanta, GA, and Georgia State University, also in Atlanta. He and his wife, Mary, live in the Atlanta area, serving the Lord faithfully.

Table of Contents

Jesus Feeds the People (detail)

I Would be Telling You

I would be telling you
Of rainbows… feet unshod,
A hiding of the face
For fear of seeing God.

I would be telling you
God's story and ours, too:
The mystery of our lives
Entwined with heaven's blue.

I would be telling you
The gospel in two parts—
First then, in Galilee;
Again, within our hearts.

I would be telling you
The Tale I cannot tell,
The Word, past speech, our God
With us, Immanuel.

Agur's Riddle

Who has gone up to heaven
and come down?
Who has gathered up the wind
in the hollow of his hands?
Who has wrapped up the waters
in his cloak?
Who has established
all the ends of the earth?
What is his Name,
and the name of his Son?
Tell me if you know!

Proverbs 30:4, from the NIV

Moses and the Burning Bush:

Exodus 3:1-14

Why was the bush burning and not consumed?
Why did Moses turn aside?

This Moses—
Had the old desire to free God's people flickered out and died?
Was Moses content or at least reconciled to the idea
of keeping Jethro's sheep for the rest of his life
in that waste howling wilderness?

Was his own life like a bush in the desert, dried and withered,
or maybe even green, but not aflame?
Or had the bush in his soul caught fire in his earlier years,
Blazed with mighty words and deeds,
Only to be reduced to ashes in the land of exile,
A stranger in a strange land?

Or did he consider himself a stranger
because there was something still smoldering in his bosom,
a fire inside that others around him seemed to lack?

Why did Moses turn aside?
Was it the curiosity of a phenomenologist: "Ah, what is this new sight?"
Or did something in the bush speak
to the smoking flax deep in his own heart?

Did the man whose history had been consumed
Find something appealing about this shrub, rooted in the earth,
Enduring the flames that danced on its leaves and clothed its branches?

Why was the bush burning and not consumed?
Does it represent Israel doomed to suffer the fires of persecution
And yet not perish?

Was it a heavenly shrub,
An escape from Eden, phosphorescing in the volatile air?

What fueled the fire?
Was the bush like a wick,
drawing by its roots from some subterranean source of oil?

Had the bush an eternal quality that would not be consumed,
that refused to be 'ashes to ashes,'
that was exempt from creation's bondage to decay?

Was the bush from heaven and the fire from earth?
Or were both from heaven?
Or both from earth?
Or was the bush from earth and fire from heaven?

Did the bush not burn up because the fire was gentle in its ways
refusing to hurt the green leaves and twigs?

Did the bush flame with that Pentecostal fire that would rest on the disciples
and cause words to be spoken
that had never been voiced quite like that before?
God's intercom in the desert!
Leaves and twigs burning merrily—
Trembling with the fire and the Word!

Moses and the Burning Bush

What Shepherds Saw

Wrapped in swaddling clothes,
Lying in a manger…
What did shepherds go forth to see?
While priests ministered in the temple
And dared not go behind the veil,
Shepherds came into the Holy Place
And looked through a veil of swaddling clothes
To see a newborn baby
Lying in a manger,
The song of the armies of heaven
Still echoing within their hearts,
"Glory to God in the highest
And on earth, peace, goodwill toward men!"

But the song gave place to the child
Lying in the manger,
To Him who had rent the heavens
And had come down…
The mountains in hearts
Flowed down at His presence:
At Him who had emptied Himself
And had come down
And was dwelling among us.

For though He had poured Himself out,
He did not lose who He is
And that was what shone forth
As clear as the morning star on a cloudless dawn
And was the Light of all people.

Shepherds who before had only heard song
Gave birth to a song themselves,
Glorifying and praising God
At the sight of the baby,
Just like any other baby—
But as Adam was Adam
And Seth was Seth
And Cain was Cain,
This baby was Jesus,
The fullness of God,
Wrapped in swaddling clothes,
Lying in a manger.
Jesus.

The Shepherd from Bethlehem

But you, Bethlehem Ephratah,
though you are small among the clans of Judah,
out of you will come for me
one who will be ruler over Israel,
whose origins are from of old,
from days of eternity.
Therefore Israel shall be abandoned
until the time when she who is in labor gives birth
and the rest of his brothers return to join the Israelites.
He will stand and shepherd his flock
in the strength of the LORD,
in the majesty of the name of the LORD his God.
And they will live securely, for then his greatness
will reach to the ends of the earth.
And he will be their peace.

Micah 5:2-5a, from the NIV

The Good Shepherd, the Door for the Sheep

The Time of Waiting

What was that time of waiting like
in the household of Zechariah and Elizabeth
for the three months Mary was with them?
We could call this household the first church—
the first gathering of believers.
Of all the people in the world,
these three were the only ones who knew the truth.

What a gift Elizabeth was to Mary!
Mary knew that she was facing misunderstanding, reproach and trouble,
but here at the beginning she had an older loved one
who believed in her and honored her.
Did John leap within Elizabeth again after that first encounter?
I suspect he did, reminding his mother how special was her guest!

And how did Zechariah process Mary's visit?
I can imagine it. Mary shows up.
She and Elizabeth have a wonderful exchange:
Elizabeth prophesies; Mary sings her "Magnificat."
But this is all a pantomime to Zechariah.
He beholds it like a silent movie with no subtitles.
So he hands his little wax writing tablet to Elizabeth,
"Who is she?"
"She is my cousin."
"Who?"
"Mary. The daughter of Eli from Nazareth."
"Why is she here?"
"God sent her."
"Oh?"
"Yes."
"Why?"
"She's pregnant."

"Really?"

"Yes."

"The angel Gabriel came to visit her, too."

"O Holy One of Israel, have mercy on us!"

"Yes, and he told her that she would bear the Messiah."

"Really?!?!"

"Yes."

"Do you believe her?"

"Yes, I do. After all, look at us!"

"True, true…"

"And not only that—our baby leaped within me when Mary entered—
he already knows who Mary is carrying!"

"O Most High, please forgive me…"

The good news begins to sink into Zechariah's heart;
day by day, he becomes more and more a believer.

So the old couple and the young woman adjust to daily living,
there in that household, during this time of waiting and gestation.
The neighbors know something special is going on with Elizabeth,
but no one suspects that her miracle can hardly be compared
to the miracle taking place within the young stranger from Nazareth.
Did Elizabeth ever talk with Mary about what it was like
to live with reproach, year after year in a small town?
I'm sure they rejoiced and sang of victory and the Coming of the Lord.
But mostly they took comfort in one another's company,
engaging in all the tasks of expecting a child in a normal household.
Did Zechariah keep to himself or did he pass his tablet
to Elizabeth from time to time to join in the conversation?
Did he ever hand his tablet to Mary?

The time of waiting and "normal living" would be a gift in itself,
especially for Mary who would be facing so much upheaval and disruption.

She would be able to draw on this time of calm and understanding,
of waiting and hoping, of mutual respect and caring…
This time of waiting would become a reservoir deep within,
the season when she got into the habit of pondering,
trusting, and letting God work his work.
She could wander back in her mind to the hill country of Judea
and remember that there was an old couple raising a lively son,
who knew her, believed in her and prayed for her.
And as she pondered so many things in her heart,
this couple would serve as an anchor in her imagination,
proof that those who waited upon the Lord,
would renew their strength, mount up with wings as eagles,
run, and not be weary, walk, and not faint.

The Annunciation

Pioneer

Like a divine Gulliver,
Like the sole survivor of a shipwreck,
God's Son once found himself washed up on the shores of our humanity.

In making his way back to God,
He made a way for us all.

This One who pioneered our salvation
Invites us to take up the heavenly odyssey, saying,
"I am the Way, the Truth and the Life,
No one comes to the Father except through me."

Listen to the Shepherds

Luke 2:8-20

We spent our nights with the eternal silences,
the deep dome of heaven lit with all the multitudes of stars.
Did we ever consider that God Almighty
had looked at that same sky with Abraham our father,
that the upward look into the infinite
was as close as you could get
toward seeing the extent of God's promise?
Who among us had ever counted all the stars?

The vast depth of heaven did not oppress us
as it might some proud soul
threatened by forces, and light and joy beyond his control or ken.
We considered the heavens and felt quite small,
But it was a comfort because we knew
we were small and that our God was greater
than all the greatness stretched above us.

We had our place and it was a low one and we accepted it.
Yes, David was a shepherd,
and so were Abraham, Isaac and Jacob.
But now our calling, Bible known and Bible honored,
was no longer honored by those who taught in synagogue and temple
because we hardly ever came to hear them.
We couldn't—we were out in the fields night and day.
We could not keep the Sabbath as closely
as those who dwelt in town and village,
who honored the shepherds of the Bible
but despised us as men on the margins of God's salvation.

We had heard the story from the Scriptures,
told around the campfire,
of David, little regarded by his brothers, relegated to keeping sheep,
away from the important happenings of the family and the town.
Yet he was called and compelled to come
to the feast by the prophet Samuel
who refused to sit down and eat before he came.
But no one would wait for us;
none troubled that we were not at table.

No matter—these fields were David's fields;
these glens and pastures were grazed by David's sheep.
This night sky was David's sky a thousand years ago.
These hills had heard the sweet singer of Israel
as much or more than the walls of Bethlehem town had.

Only once were we called to come to Bethlehem.
Only once did we leave our flocks like David did
in response to a divine summons—only once,
when the Angel of the Lord stepped out of David's sky
and stood shining in the night
and confided to us news of a great gladness
which would not be limited to a certain caste or race
but would be for all people.

We trembled and quaked as we stood before the angel,
but he comforted us and said, "Fear not!"
Those words still live within us like the walls of a strong fortress.
We heard with our own ears the glad tidings
that a Savior had just been born in Bethlehem—
that the Lord Messiah had come at last.
The angel gave us a sign to look for:
a Baby wrapped in swaddling clothes and lying in a manger.

As wonder upon wonder from on high tumbled down
upon our hearts with this great news,
(The meaning of it all hardly beginning to sink in),
suddenly great companies of the forces of heaven stood with the angel.
Like the sound of many waters,
armies of angels sang in perfect unison in our dialect,
with such joy and triumph, such worship and fierce love to God
that their unforgettable song shall always ring in our hearts:
"Glory to God in the highest
and on earth peace, good will to all people!"

The angel did not command us to go and see the Child,
but the news was irresistible.
Otherwise why would he have given us the sign?
He knew we would go and seek for Him.
When the angels were gone we talked it over.
Surely the Lord had called us to go and see.
So we went and looked where we thought He might be.
The sign implied He would not be in a normal house,
so we checked the stables we knew.
Checking stables was easier than knocking on doors
in the middle of the night.

As shepherds, we had all looked for stray sheep
but that was out in the wild, and this was in town.
As we drew near we had the sense
that things were not what they seemed to be,
that somehow they were reversed:
that we were the ones who were lost—
that in seeking the Child we were looking for our Shepherd.
When we saw Him lying in the manger
it was as if we had been found.

Wondering, Joseph and Mary received us into the stable.
It was set into a hill with a cave at the back.

It was filled with the usual inhabitants:
a cow, a donkey, a milking goat, a couple of sheep
and a few doves and pigeons in the rafters.
There on one side, in a place swept and strewn with new straw,
was the young Mother lying down on a pallet,
exhausted from childbirth and a long journey,
and her Husband standing by the Child in the manger.
We told them of the glad tidings of the angel.
We begged forgiveness for the intrusion
but felt we had been summoned to come and see.
The couple gave each other knowing looks
and Joseph smiled and said, yes,
he reckoned we had been called to come.
The awkwardness gave way to worship
as we knelt before our new born King—
Our Shepherd come to claim us.

To keep them from the cold,
we gave them some of our blankets
woven from the wool of our sheep.
We gave Mary curds made from the milk of our sheep
And some of the bread we were accustomed to eating in the fields.

We have seen many newborn babies in our time,
And newborn lambs without count
And every entrance into this world is a marvel and a wonder.
But this was different.
It was as if within this cave
the heavens opened in a greater way
than the night sky that had just held the heavenly host
and had shone with God's glory.
Here in this stable the heavens were truly opened.

And something in our hearts opened as well.
Now we began to sing and to praise God,
Now we were joining with the heavenly choir!

This newborn Baby lying in a manger
(just as the angel had told us)
unlocked the gates of our hearts
and opened the doors of our mouths.

The angel made us seekers,
But the Child made us messengers.
After seeing Him,
We couldn't help but praise and glorify our God—
we couldn't help but tell anyone who would listen
of all that we had seen and heard.

We had thought that we had been excluded from the feast,
but God opened heaven and found us where we were
on that hillside outside Bethlehem
and used angels to invite us into town
and though there was little ordinary food that night,
our hearts have been feasting ever since
on the great banquet spread for us
in the coming of our Savior.

He has made us His messengers to all,
even to those who feel stuck out on a hillside somewhere,
stranded on the nightshift—who feel their place in this life
somehow excludes them from coming to the feast.

When our Lord Jesus came to us all
that cold, wondrous and starry night so long ago,
He spread a table that would fill us with the life of God—
He prepared a feast to which all may come.
Come, all things are now ready!

The Shepherds Worship the Baby

Good News

When the Eternal Majesty
Was tucked inside the frame of a small Boy,
God said something about Himself
That we desperately needed to hear—
Good News!

"And she brought forth her firstborn Son … and laid him in a manger."

The Battle is God's

"Do not be afraid or discouraged because of this vast army.
For the battle is not yours but God's."
2 Chronicles 20:15

What a sight they must have been!
Imagine going into battle
And making the choir the vanguard!
But the Hebrew king knew they were outnumbered
And knew that Judah must rely on the Lord.
As they sought the Lord, the prophet spoke,
"Do no be afraid or discouraged because of this vast army.
For the battle is not yours but God's."
They could not win against their foes through strength of arms.
And so they appointed singers to go before the army.
Their battle cry and song of victory was,
"Give thanks to the Lord,
For His steadfast love endures forever!"

As they began to sing and praise,
The Lord set ambushes against the enemies of Judah
To ambush each other and fight each other
Until no one was left.
And it took three days for the soldiers of Judah
To pick their way through the dead bodies and carry off the spoils.

All this took place
In the Pass of Ziz and the Desert Jeruel,
About ten or fifteen miles south of the hill country
Surrounding the little town of Bethlehem,
Where some eight centuries later,
Armies would be gathered again.
Only this time it would be the 'multitude of the heavenly host.'

What a sight they must have been!
Imagine going into battle
And making the choir the vanguard!
Ah, but this battle the angels had no hope of winning,
Neither through strength of arms nor through spiritual might.
For the disputed territory was the soul of humanity
And the ground of battle was the human heart.
So they stood by the passes in the heavens
And sang over the deserts of our barren hills,
And worshipped the Lord God of Hosts,
Who was making this battle that they could not fight—His!

Their battle cry and song of victory was,
"Glory to God in the highest!
And on earth, peace, goodwill among people!"
And the Lord of Hosts waded into the fray
At just the right time,
When both heaven and earth were powerless—
When neither could reclaim captive humanity from the Enemy.
When death and hell, sin and Satan,
Sorrow and desolation, malignant principalities and archons,
Evil and our own corruption, our own guilt and folly—
When all these were allied against us…

The Lord began to lay ambushes against them
In this Baby born of the Virgin Mary,
Wrapped in swaddling clothes and lying a manger.
Now on the ground of our own humanity
God Himself took up our struggle
In Jesus, the King of Glory,
The Lord strong and mighty,
The Lord mighty in battle.

So He was tempted in all points like we are.
In all the points where we have sinned and failed and fallen short,
From His first conscious choices as a child
To His final choices in the garden
And on the bloody Tree,
He never sinned.

Jesus won every battle that we lost.
He was faithful and true where we were not.
He was considerate where we could have cared less.
He was chaste where we were impure.
He was brave where we were full of fear.
He brought healing with both word and touch
Where we had left wounds and scars.
He loved—loved both God and people
When we were full of fear and hate and indifference.

All the ancient allies and enemies took their turns at Him
And none could vanquish Him.
Even when they gathered round Him on that final day
At the edge of the world
And considered that they had won—
In His weakness and seeming folly
The Lord of Hosts laid ambushes for them all—
And they defeated themselves at the cross,
As they dashed themselves against His incorruptible righteousness,
Against His utter and infinite integrity,
Like monsters of the deep crashing against a great Rock in a storm.

Did it take three days for the heavenly host, the Lord's armies,
To gather up the spoils of the victory
And then parade them in triumphal procession
When Jesus rose in power from the grave?

"Glory to God in the highest!
And on earth, peace, goodwill among people!"
"Glad tidings which shall be to all people!"
For the Lord Himself has turned back our enemies
And He has won within our humanity
The great victory when He came and dwelt among us,
And gave His life upon the tree,
And rose triumphant from death.
"Give thanks to the Lord,
For His steadfast love endures forever!"

The Temptation in the Wilderness

They Shall See God

Matthew 3

John the Baptist was an eye doctor standing in the wilderness,
Crying, "Repent, for the Kingdom of Heaven is at hand!"
But John did not deal with eyes;
He dealt with hearts.

> Blessed are the pure in heart
> For they shall see God.

People came to him in the deserted places by the River Jordan,
Burdened by their past, regretting their sins
Knowing they were not fit to receive the Coming King.

We tend to picture John as an austere holiness preacher
Clothed in camel's hair and eating whatever was at hand,
Wild honey from the combs in the rock
And locusts or grasshoppers,
A fearsome character straight out of Central Casting.

We forget how the preaching of John
Not only convicted people of their sins,
But gave those same people hope!
He brought relief and healing.
They did not have to remain burdened and full of regret.
They could make a new start;
They could wash away their sins in Jordan's River
And come out clean and whole
And ready for the Coming King.

For this King would not be known by the seeing of the eye,
But by the seeing of the heart:

> Blessed are the pure in heart
> For they shall see God.

So they came to this eye doctor,
This Voice crying in the wilderness
And the valleys of despair were lifted up;
The mountains and hills of pride were made low.
The crooked ways that obscured their vision were made straight,
And the rough places were made plain.

When the Glory of the Lord came down to the Jordan
And seemed to be like all the other repentant sinners
Going into the water and submitting to John's baptism—
When Jesus of Nazareth stood there before John,
And the heavens opened and some thought it thundered—
When those who refused John's prescription for their hearts
Saw only a man soaking wet from being baptized,
These who had repented,
These who had let John purify their hearts,
These were truly blessed—
For they saw God!

Epiphany—Jesus and John the Baptist

Jacob, You Dreamer!

Genesis 28:10-22; John 1:43-51

Jacob, you dreamer! With your eyes closed tight
How dared you see so clearly in the night
What you never saw in day's fair light?
You who listened to your mother
And through your father's blind twilight
Did outwit him and elder brother,
Could you yet be blessed by Him who ever sees—
In grace receive at outset of your quest
Enough for you and all earth's families
To be blessed?

Jacob, you dreamer! Was it you who dreamed
Or was your dream a gift, a loan from on high?
As you laid your head upon the stone,
Your ear pressed close against the earth,
Did you hear her homesick moan?
Or was it just your own road-weary sigh?
As you slept and listened to the earth
Did you hear creation's groan
Or heaven's birth?

Jacob, you dreamer! Whose dream did you dream
When you saw heaven and earth reconciled by the stair
That stretched from your pillow to God's throne?
Could He who neither slumbers nor sleeps yet have dreamed
Of free concourse between heaven opened and a world redeemed?
Did this dream keep you in all your ways,
A promise from on high of fellowship to be true
From the God of Abraham and Isaac
And now you?

Jacob, you dreamer! Whose sons were climbing
Those steps to heaven and returning?
Were they heaven's sons or sons of earth?
Were they your sons who mounted up that stair
And lived their lives of toil and hope and care?
Were they heaven's pioneers, pilgrims in the earth?
Were they heirs of a desire, a hope, a gleam,
A longing nurtured from birth, guarded, carried,
A blessing, a curse, for better, for worse—married
To a dream?

Jacob, you dreamer! Were you aware
The dreams of all were climbing up that stair,
Ascending up and coming down to beckon, to plead
With all mankind and staunch the need,
Until the time when coming in God's plan
Your wondrous stair becomes a Man?
And were there echoes of the call to "Come and see?"
Nathanael running from underneath the fig tree—
A promise of angels ascending and descending on God's Lamb,
And the marvelous voice of Jesus saying, "I am
All you ever longed for; all that God wants too:
The dream come true."

Jesus and Nathanael

The Light of the World

John 8:12-30

Lord Jesus, what would you have said if you had not been interrupted?
What would you have told us about your being the Light of the world?
You said that if we followed you, we would have the Light of life.
Oh, Lord, evermore, give us your Light!
For with you is the fountain of life; in your Light we see light.

But what would you have told us?
Would you have said something like this?
"I am the Light that shines in the darkness of this world.
The darkness cannot overcome it, cannot overshadow my Light,
cannot overpower my Light, cannot comprehend the Light that I am.
The Light that shines from me is the Light of my life.

"I am the Light that shines through my single human life.
Mine is the Light of the Word made flesh.
In order to rescue the souls trapped in darkness,
those living in the land of the shadow of death,
I have come down, not as the sun to obliterate all shadows,
(That will come! But not now)—
I have come down from the light of Heaven
(where my uncreated Light outshines all other lights
and is the incandescent heart, the source of all the lights of heaven)—
I have come down to shine in the realm of the Shadow
in such a way that I may love people into Life!

That by my life, my words, my works of power,
a Light will shine in the darkness of their hearts
that will not destroy them, but save them,
rescue them, retrieve their own calling to walk in my Light
and have fellowship with me and with the Father—
in whom there is no darkness at all!

"Now I call you to follow me in loving God and loving people.
When you do, you also shall shine in your own peculiar ways,
and shall be a city on a hill, shining with my Light to the world."

And God said, "Let there be light!"

Coming To

I was but dust before you came—
Scattered, empty, lost and lame,
Your image marred beyond recall,
Myself forgot, and that was all
Because I had forgotten you.

And yet you came and by your birth
Gave scattered dust a priceless worth;
Made human life a sacred charge
(The Word in letters written large)
Because I needed what was true

To rescue me from living lies,
To tell me that it's me you prize,
If I my secret self would give
To you and turn and truly live,
Because I live by knowing you.

For I was blind in willful night,
Could not conceive the realm of sight,
But like the prodigal came to
Myself and then came home to you.
I found myself by finding you.

Oh Jesus, how could I forget
Your coming to this world—and yet
To keep my heart from growing cold
Must hear your story Scripture told—
Because I must remember you.

Lord Jesus, thank you that you came
And of our lives, partook the same
Heartache and delight that goes
With being human and this shows
Our praise: a remembering of you.

The Treader of the Deep

John 6:16-21

I have this impression of a great Figure
walking in the moonlight,
treading on the waves of the sea.
His purpose is his own;
no one can alter it, not even the chaotic forces of the deep.
He lets the wind blow his hair
and flutter his robes—but he rules it nonetheless.

I see him walking on the sea, treading the waves
as if they were solid and could bear him up.
He commands the slippery elements to give traction to his feet,
to be what they are not, purely for his purpose.
The touch of his feet gives the water its solidity
just long enough to bear him to the next footfall
and then it recedes back into its original state,
once Jesus takes that next step.
He who caused the waters of the Red Sea
to congeal and rest in a wall on either side
as the children of Israel passed through on the ocean bottom,
now causes the waters to congeal beneath him
just long enough for him to take the next step.
Everything in creation must submit to his purpose.
All things work together to bear him up
on the waves and in the troughs
as he marches to the rescue of those he loves.

I see our Lord Jesus walking on the troubled deep,
stepping surely and confidently as the King of glory.
He is the Lord of hosts, mighty in battle;
not a battle of revolution the Five Thousand wanted,

but the Victor of the battle of the human heart at the cross,
where the Lord trampled down sin and Satan, hell and death,
regret and sorrow, pain and suffering,
even as he treads on the uncontrollable forces of chaos,
the turmoil of the waves in the night on Galilee.

So the Lord sends away
the crowd who wanted to make him king.
And he sets his face as a flint
and treads the path toward Golgotha.
He will tread that path though his footprints are not seen.
He moves in his own time
and in his own mysterious purpose,
the King of a far greater realm than any could conceive,
walking in the will of his Father to save us
and rescue us from perishing in the deep.
He comes to us in the middle of our night,
when we are exhausted and afraid,
and don't know which end is up,
when it seems like we have been getting nowhere,
and speaks to us in the language of home and belonging,
"It is I! Don't be afraid!"

Jesus Walks on the Water with a Modern-Day Disciple

Love Riding on the Ridiculous

Matthew 21:1-11

Love came riding into their lives on the ridiculous.
He came amid shouts and cries
Of those who knew nothing
But that He had bidden a friend from death to life
And that He did not refuse being called
The Son of David.

So the true Hebrew king would be known—
Not on horses of Egypt or Rome
But on a donkey, an ass or the foal of an ass.
Just as their first kings were known,
So the last would recall the first
When the promise to David was fulfilled.

The prophets sensed and knew—
They foretold to the Daughter of Zion
How He would come,
So that she would not miss
The things that belonged to her peace—
Ah! But she missed them anyway.

And we who sing, "Hosanna,"
Have we learned the lesson yet?
The treasure is in the pot of clay;
The Almighty on the absurd,
Love riding on the ridiculous—
The ridiculous news that our sins are forgiven,
And that He is not ashamed of us.

We cannot embarrass Him
Who took upon Himself our foolishness.
He will own us if we will own Him
Who had mercy on our absurdity,
Accepting praise from those who knew no better
And scorn from those who thought they did.

Jesus Laments over Jerusalem (detail)

The Stark Solitude of His Love

"Imagine what it was like before creation, before the angels, before anything was made, seen or unseen—just God—in the stark solitude of his love."
Paul Sexton

In the vast everlasting before he began
Creating the universe, the angels and man,
God was, always was and continued to be
Just himself, who he is in primordial glory.
'Twas a time beyond time, before mountain or hill,
Where as yet there was naught for All-presence to fill,
No thing for Omnipotence to rule or to will,
Not a thing for Omniscience to know and yet still

He was God before light, time and space
Or Satan or angels or human race,
Before all powers or death or life
Or heavenly war or earthly strife,
Before he did move on the face of the deep,
Or fashioned the heavens, his castle and keep.
He was God before all beneath or above,
In the stark solitude of his love.

Oh, the vast everlasting before earth was wild…
Are reflections of that in the face of a Child?
In the humbling of God to become what we are—
What he's like at the core was revealed 'neath the star,
At a time beyond time under Bethlehem's hill,
Nowhere else but a manger for his presence to fill,
Naught for his omnipotence to rule or to will,
When he did not know much—just a babe and yet still

The same God as before light, time or space
Only local, confined in the human race,
The same as before all powers or death,
'Mid heavenly song and earthly breath,
Only now he had moved upon Mary's new deep
And fashioned a Man, his castle and keep;
The fulfillment of all beneath and above,
Christ, the stark solitude of his love.

Ah, the vast everlasting before he began…
Are disclosures of that in the face of a Man?
In the face of a Man so beaten and bruised,
Rejected of men and spitefully used
At a time beyond time upon Calvary's hill,
When 'twas naught but a cross for his presence to fill,
No one else but himself to rule or to will,
When he did not know much but our plight and yet still

The same God as before light, time or space,
Only more so, revealed in the human race,
Defeating all powers and death with life,
Past heavenly war and earthly strife.
Now he did move on humanity's deep
And fashioned the church, his castle and keep,
As he hung between all that's beneath or above—
In the stark solitude of his love.

Has the vast everlasting before he began,
Ever blazed on your heart in the face of this Man?
Has the glory that dwelt in the Father's own Son

Transfigured your life with the triumph he won?
A persuasion that springs from a time beyond time
And is filled with his presence convincing the mind
That he rules in your heart because he was kind
And gave all that he knew that your life he might find.

For I am persuaded neither light, time or space,
Nor Satan, nor angels, nor human race,
Nor princes, nor powers, nor death, nor life,
Nor heavenly war, nor earthly strife
Can separate us from his love so deep—
For he's fashioned himself our castle and keep:
Things beneath can't part us, nor things above,
From the stark solitude of his love.

A Strange New Pass

Heaven and earth how far apart!
How different and strange from each other!
Reflections obscured by an absurd art
Are found in earth's tragic mirror.

Like a beautiful tree that caresses the sky
With limbs and leaves full of grace,
So the heavenly realm is wonderfully high
With a beauty that brightens the face.

There the Son of God reigns from a glorious throne
And he rides on a marvelous steed
And bright hosts in white make his praise known
While mounted they follow his lead.

There the Tree of Life grows its fruit to impart
Food and Life from the victory won.
There Life's river flows from heaven's bright heart:
The throne of God and his Son.

But the beautiful tree which caresses the sky
Has its roots deep down in the earth.
In the twists and the gnarls God himself drew nigh
And gave life a strange new worth.

When God came down through the Savior's birth
We hid our faces from his,
For heaven brought down and declared in earth
Is not what we think it is.

For the heavenly glory is not to be found
In the palace of kings or Caesar's throne,
But God is a Man who trudges the ground
'Neath the weight of the world that he bears all alone.

Here Life's river flows from heaven's bright heart
In Christ's side that was pierced by the spear,
And whoever wills may drink for his part
Freely, what to God was so dear.

Oh earth, we've come to a strange new pass
Where the glorious steed is a humble ass,
Where heaven's triumph is an earthly loss
And the throne of God is an earthly cross.

If I Be Lifted Up

John 12:32

"And I, if I be lifted up, will draw all men to me."
His lifting up in death he meant, and spoke of Calvary.

For as a star's collapse in death creates an unseen core
That draws all things unto itself, so Christ's death even more

Exerts a pull on everyone—on things in heaven and earth,
And by its sway holds all in place by Jesus' moral worth.

The pull of Christ upon the cross the world may oft resist;
Still he's the center that will hold—"By him all things consist."

The universe revolves around this core of sacrifice:
The dying Man and dying God, redemption's full paid price.

Be glad, for Heaven from its heart is ruled by love's great act!
The cross's dying Lamb now sits enthroned by this great fact.

So time and space must bow the knee—yes, all created things,
Acknowledge Jesus Christ as Lord, Love's wounded King of kings.

.

A Man in the Rain

When light breaks through from the side of the skies
And finds itself caught and impaled and it dies
In the rain that descends from the dark cloud above,
A rainbow is seen, a sign of God's love.

Oh, the colors were there in the light all along
But only the rain can bring out the song
That's been sung by the Glory around heaven's throne:
Light's manifold nature displayed and made known.

When the ark came to rest on Ararat's horn
And Noah went forth into mankind's new morn,
God's judgment drew back with the storm on the wane
And his mercy shone forth in the sunlight's new reign.

These two seeming foes did meet in the bow
That was set in the clouds God's promise to show
Both to him and to us the witness of light
That's been caught in the rain, making peace of the fight.

Has your heart ever looked with wonder and awe
At the bow in the cloud and sensed more than you saw
In the judgment and mercy that met in the rain
And looked beyond that to the Lamb that was slain?

Look—a man just like us who lived life in our shade
And by that pure life a pure light he displayed
That shone with compassion and candor and grace
From Bethlehem's manger to the skull's awful place—

And there did God's wrath and his love fully meet
Finding perfect fulfillment: a Work that's complete.
The whole spectrum of love through sorrow and pain
Was declared unto us by a Man in the rain.

Why the Darkness?

At the sixth hour darkness came over the whole land until the ninth hour.
Mark 15:33.

Why is it, Lord, that when you were giving your life upon the tree,
The earth grew dark?
Did the crickets sing or did a hush settle over the land?
Did the railers and mockers grow quiet?
Or were their voices tinged with fear?

What did the darkness mean?

Were you paying the penalty for our sins?
Was it the shadow of the iniquity of us all being laid on you?
Was it the sin of the world that blotted out the sun?

Or did the forces of night gather round the cross
To gloat and animate the scorn of those who passed by?
Was this the shadow of spiritual wickedness, rulers and dominions
Who thought that at last they had you in their power—
In their hour and power of darkness?
Was this sin and Satan, hell and death
Taking up their thrones at the place of the skull?

Did your light shine even in this darkness?
Was the light of your life, your character, your nature such
That the darkness could not overpower it?
Could not comprehend it?
Did the ancient serpent strike your heel
And smash his head on your righteousness and innocence,
Your infinitely substantial Deity?

Or was the blinding of the sun, creation's modesty
That dared not look upon your nakedness?

Golgotha—The Sixth Hour

And when she saw you desolate and exposed,
Did the sun for shame refuse to shine upon this crime
So terrible against you that the earth trembled and the rocks rent?

Was the darkness the cloak the Father wrapped around you
While the soldiers gambled for the clothes
That they had stripped from you?
Was this darkness the shadow of the Almighty,
The secret place of the Most High?

Was this darkness the effect of the grieving of the Father—
Was it that the Father could not bear to look upon your suffering?
In all your affliction, was he afflicted?

O Word made flesh!
Is this the darkness of the Holy of Holies
Where all natural lights are extinguished
And only the glory shines above the mercy seat?
You who sit enthroned between the cherubim,
Are you now enthroned between two thieves?
May we see your glory here?
Is the glory that we see here the revelation of your Person?
Is this the glory of the Only-begotten of the Father,
Full of grace and truth?
Should we take our shoes off?
Are we standing on holy ground?

Was this darkness the prelude to a new creation?
Were we like the troubled deep—
Lost, without form and void?
Were you, O Spirit of God, brooding on the face of the waters
There at Calvary in the dark, making ready for the Word—
Making ready for the light to shine in our hearts?

Is the darkness here because this is the place of the hidden God?
Would it be like the darkness at Sinai where Moses received the covenant?
Is the darkness simply there as the substance of our blindness?
Does it adumbrate not only all we do not know of you,
But also all we cannot know of you,
Coming down in all your impenetrability?
And coming out of the Crucified in the same manner—
Working a work of unfathomable dimensions and repercussions?

Is this your inner or central frontier,
O God, in the terrible Trinity of your being
Which we cannot see and so seeming dark to us—
But there forging a new covenant for the house of Israel
Now subsumed in the world's unbelief and blindness,
The world that you so love that you give your Only-begotten
In order have mercy upon us all?

Is this the secret into which only you, Heavenly Father, can see?
Ah! And shall you, who see in secret, reward your Son openly,
Infinitely and everlastingly, in love and honour?

As we seek to peer into this darkness
Are we seeking to look into the depth
Of the riches of the wisdom and knowledge of God?
Do we have here before us your unsearchable judgments,
Your paths which are beyond tracing out?
Is this where we cannot know the mind of the Lord?
And who here would even dream of being your counsellor?
And how could we ever repay you for what you are doing?
Have we stumbled here on the nexus where
From you and through you and to you are all things?

Oh Jesus, take my life
And hide me here with you!
Draw me with the drawing
That only you can do:

Be my sacrifice for sin—
My victory over Night;
Be my comfort deep within
The Shadow of your Light!

And if I grope in blindness
And stumble in the dark
My hope shall be your kindness
If I should touch the Ark.

There let me find your Mercy Seat
The lowly hidden throne
Where all your powers and tempers meet,
Resolve, and claim your own.

What Did Jesus Say?

Luke 24:13-32

What did Jesus say on the way to Emmaus?
How did he open the minds and hearts
of those two brokenhearted disciples?
What was "all that the prophets have spoken?"

Did Jesus tell of Adam and the deep sleep
and the Lord God reaching into his side
and taking a rib and forming a bride for him?
Did he tell of how the Lord God
reached into the riven side of the Son of Man
and formed a bride for him while he slept in death?
Did Jesus tell of the promise to Eve how her offspring
would bruise the serpent's head
and the serpent cause him suffering as well?

Did he tell the real meaning of sacrifice—
how all of it was a foreshadowing of his own sacrifice?
Did he tell them how he had atoned for our sins?
Did Jesus tell of the mountains of Moriah,
a father offering his son, the voice from heaven,
the ram caught in the thicket and—
his own head tangled in a crown of thorns?
Did he tell of Joseph's humiliation and betrayal
and how he brought salvation to his family
and to the very brothers who sold him into slavery?
Did he say that what men meant for evil,
God meant for good—the saving of many lives?

Did Jesus tell them of Moses and Pharaoh and the Passover lamb?
Did he tell these two disciples who had lost hope,
how God had heard the cry of his people in bondage
and had come down to deliver them

from a far more terrible tyrant than Pharaoh?
Did Jesus tell them of the parting of the waters of the Red Sea
and how he had parted the waters of death
with his own death and resurrection?
Did he tell them of Moses
lifting up the serpent in the wilderness
and that all who looked on it
should be healed from serpent's poison—
and how all who looked the Son of Man being lifted up
would be healed of the poison of sin
and would not perish, but have everlasting life?

Did he remind them that a prophet like Moses would come
and do the very things
that Moses only outlined in type and shadow?
Did Jesus tell them of the Tabernacle
and God dwelling among his people
and that at the heart of heaven is the Mercy Seat
and how that Mercy Seat became incarnate
in the Lord of Glory giving his life upon the tree?
Did he tell of entrance into the holiest
by a new and living way—
the way of his dying on the cross?

Did he tell how he brought us out of the land of bondage
to bring us into the Promised Land,
a land flowing with milk and honey?
Did he tell of Joshua,
the warrior with his own name,
causing the sun to stand still
and winning the victory for God's people
and how the sun withdrew its shining
when he was on the cross,
conquering the hosts of hell for us all?

Did Jesus tell them about love and loyalty,
righteousness and peace,
in the story of his ancestors, Ruth and Boaz?
Did he tell of David and all his troubles,
and how he suffered rejection from his own people
before he came into the kingdom and the throne?

Did he tell of Job longing for a Redeemer?
Did he speak of the Suffering Servant in Isaiah?
And tell of the Righteous Branch in Jeremiah?
Did Jesus tell how by his death and resurrection
he had made a New Covenant for a New Israel?
Did he tell of the valley of dry bones in Ezekiel
and how he would bring hope
to those whose hope was lost?
Did he tell of the new name of the city of God,
The Lord Is There,
and how he brought this to pass
by his own Incarnation, suffering and death?

Did he tell how those who will be true to God
will end up in the fiery furnace,
as Daniel's friends found out,
but that they also found fellowship
with a fourth man in the fire—
the Son of God himself?
And that he is that fourth man
who is well acquainted with suffering?

Did Jesus tell of Hosea redeeming of an unfaithful wife
and how the Lord had done the same
on the cross with wayward Israel?
Did he tell how his death on the cross
would open the floodgates of heaven
so that God would pour out his Spirit as Joel foretold?

The Resurrection

Did Jesus tell how he took injustice upon himself at the cross
so that, as Amos foretold in his protest,
justice could roll down like a river,
and righteousness like a never-failing stream?

Did he tell how Obadiah foresaw deliverance on Mount Zion,
the coming of God's kingdom
and how he, Jesus,
was fulfilling this in his death and resurrection?
Did he tell of the sign of the prophet Jonah
who plunged into the heart of the sea in the belly of the whale
and how he, Jesus, had fulfilled that sign
by plunging into death and into the heart of the earth
and now was alive again?
If Nineveh believed Jonah,
how much more should they believe
in the Risen Son of Man?
Did Jesus tell, as Micah foretold,
that he had trodden our sins underfoot at the cross
and thereby had cast all our iniquities
into the depths of the sea?
Did he tell them, like Habakkuk,
that the just would live by faith
in what he had done at the cross?
Did he tell them as Zephaniah did,
that he was mighty to save?
Did Jesus tell them that the glory of the latter house
would be greater than the glory of the former,
just as Haggai had said?
Did he tell of the fountain opened for cleansing from sin,
as Zechariah had prophesied?
Did Jesus tell them that his work on the cross
would purify the sons of Levi, as Malachi foretold,
that they might offer to the Lord
an offering in righteousness?

And will the Lord Jesus, who took the Scriptures
and used them to interpret
his own suffering and death and entrance into glory,
now interpret your own sufferings by his own?
Can we trust him,
who bore our sins and sorrows on the tree,
to draw near to us in the midst
of our disappointments and setbacks,
our loss and our grief,
and show us by the Scriptures
the way to new life and hope in him?
And will our broken hearts burn with healing
as we hear how the Scriptures tell over and over
what God has done in Christ?
And will he take the bread of ordinary life
and bless it, and break it, and give it to us,
and with the giving of himself
freely give us all things—all that the prophets have spoken?
YES!

Like Thomas

John 20:24-29

"I am not like Thomas, wounds I cannot see."[1]
But Lord, my heart has eyes, has hands, and I must be
Too much like him. I need to touch your hands and reach
My hand into your side and feel the lessons it might teach.

I am your Thomas, Lord—aught else I cannot be.
Slow to know, thick of thought, absent from your first epiphany.
Is this your Spirit masquerading as a muse in my imperfect art?
These lines the stretching forth my hand to feel your beating heart?

My Lord, My God, forgive, forgive my stony blindness!
I feel the nail prints with my thumbs—my clumsiness, your kindness.
I reach my hand into your side; touch the source of my receiving
Beatitude: your soft rebuke, "And be not faithless, but believing."

---

1   This line is a quote from Gerard Manley Hopkins' translation of a poem by St. Thomas Aquinas, "Rhythmus ad SS. Sacramentum." Gardner and MacKenzie, eds. *The Poems of Gerard Manley Hopkins*, Fourth Edition. (London: Oxford, 1970), 211.

Doubting Thomas

The Ascension

Reach Hither Thy Hand

Reach hither thy hand—
Feel the heart that was broken.
Reach hither thy hand—
Touch a wound for a token.

Reach hither thy hand—
Feel the print of the nail.
Reach hither thy hand—
For the blind this is Braille.

Reach hither thy hand—
To the Lamb that was slain.
Reach hither thy hand—
Could his love be more plain?

Reach hither thy hand—
From there you were taken.
Reach hither thy hand—
Let your faith be not shaken.

Reach hither thy hand—
Your name there is written.
Reach hither thy hand—
To the Rock that was smitten.

Reach hither thy hand—
In the side of God's giver.
Reach hither thy hand—
Touch the source of Life's River.

Reach hither thy hand—
Touch the heart's open door.
Reach hither thy hand—
Fall down and adore.

Into Galilee

As they entered the tomb, they saw a young man dressed in a white robe sitting on the right side, and they were alarmed. 6 "Don't be alarmed," he said. "You are look-ing for Jesus the Nazarene, who was crucified. He has risen! He is not here. See the place where they laid him. 7 But go, tell his disciples and Peter, 'He is going ahead of you into Galilee. There you will see him, just as he told you.'"
Mark 16:5-7, NIV

This youth has good news for us!
He has the gospel for us: Jesus is not in the tomb. He has risen!
And now Jesus waits for you to catch up with him in Galilee.
There you will meet him, just as he told you before he ever went to the cross.
Jesus predicted to his disciples that they would all fall away.
He foresaw their failure, provided for it,
and gave them instructions filled with hope.
That hope is contained in Galilee and all that is associated with it.

Galilee is the place of the springtime of Jesus' ministry.
And now with his resurrection, we come to an everlasting spring.
Go meet him in Galilee!

Galilee is a place in the Spirit for every believer.
There Jesus, who is the same yesterday, today and forever,
is still doing his mighty works.
There he is still setting people free.
There he is still healing and saving people.
There he is still preaching the wonderful news of God's forgiving love.
There he is feeding the multitudes with the bread of life.
There he is still issuing the call to come and follow him.

Will you hesitate with the women about telling
what you have heard from the youth?
Will you hesitate with the story which you have heard
from this other youth named John Mark,
just because it seems to break off awkwardly?
No! Take the narrative momentum which you have gathered
from hearing Mark's Gospel and go and meet your Lord in Galilee!
He is risen! Participate with him in this ministry.
Hear the call to follow him. Be his disciple.

We want to witness his mighty works.
We want to see the compassion in his eyes
as he takes the little children on his lap and blesses them.
We want to see Jesus take authority over the works of darkness.
We want to see him heal and save people.
We want to hear him preach the wonderful news of God's forgiving love.
We want Jesus to feed the multitudes with the bread of life.
We want to respond to his call, and come and follow him.

And could it be, that this Jesus,
risen from the dead, going before us into Galilee,
will now begin to do all these things among us?
Sometimes in spite of us?
And—most incredible of all—through us?
"He is going ahead of you into Galilee.
There you will see him, just as he told you."

My Brother's Portrait of St. Paul

IN FREE VERSE

Like a mountain in the sunlight
Whose roots reach down to dark and distant valleys,
The bald head glows
With the Glory which shines from above.
In a reclining profile,
His aged face, piercing eye, and great hooked nose
Rise from the flowing grey hair and beard
Which blend into scenes below from his life.

Below the profile, in the center, is a far younger Saul,
Knocked off his horse on the Damascus Road.
It is a time of crisis and call…
"Saul, Saul, why are you persecuting me?"
Saul replies, "Who are you, Lord?"
The Light tells him, "I am Jesus, whom you are persecuting.
It is hard for you to kick against the goads."
Stupefied, blinded, Saul reaches back and gropes for something
To try and steady himself in his world breaking apart.
What an inner revolution to realize that
Jesus is not who he wanted him to be!
That he is far other than he could have imagined!

What caught my eye when I first saw
My brother's portrait of St. Paul
Is that the Light is shining in the dark places in his life:
In the lower right, in the temple,
The Roman soldiers have to rescue him
From his rioting countrymen who are animated
By the same hate that once animated him.
That incident leads to his imprisonment
And the Light is reaching there.

In the lower left,
A great wave is washes over his pitching boat
On which he is being borne as a prisoner to Rome,
The rigging and tackling useless, loosened, or gone,
In the sea storm lasting more than a fortnight,
Ending in shipwreck and the Light is reaching there.

As I gaze at the picture,
I come back to his portrait in profile
And there he is—an old man.
He has finished his course.
He has run his race.
He has kept the faith.
His head reclines on an unseen pillow;
His grey hair is flung back;
He looks up in to the Light with a clear eye
Full of sorrow and love, joy and longing, wisdom and faith.
The eyes which once were blinded by the Light
Now see.

Ah Lord!
Grant that at my end,
I would have
My course—finished,
The race—run,
The faith—kept,
And eyes—once blinded by your Light,
Now seeing
You!

My Brother's Portrait of St. Paul

A SONNET

I see the old man, full of living, look
Up to the Light that on Damascus' road
Did blind his eyes and make his world explode:
For love, for life, he served the Light that shook

Him to the core and shining on him, took
Him through the dark, the deep, to bear the goad
That now gave peace and loosed from hearts the load
That none could, living—bear, and freed—forsook.

My brother paints him looking open-eyed
To Christ, whose splendor once did blind his sight,
But now, he looks with longing at the Light.

His race is run; the faith that he once tried
To break, he's kept—Ah, Lord, that I could see
With Paul's blind eyes life's end: to gaze on thee!

St. Paul Looking unto Jesus (detail)

Parting Thoughts from the Publisher

JESUS IS ALL IN ALL

"All things were created through Him and for Him.
He is before all things, and in Him all things hold together."
Colossians 1:16-17

There is plenty to be said and written about Christianity. Bookstores are full to overflowing with books that will help you live your best life, be happy, raise your children, save your marriage, overcome disappointment, find yourself, and get on a budget. Only a fraction of those books are about the main-event, the heart of the matter, or the core subject—Jesus.

What has drawn me to the works of this author is that he "gets it." God has illuminated Tom's heart, by his Spirit, to see Jesus revealed in Scripture, in creation, and in life. He not only recognizes that Jesus is central and universal, but he has made it his life calling to reveal Christ to others, to introduce the real Jesus to them, and to help them draw closer to him.

What, then, is our core message, the true essence of Christianity?

"Exposing the [Scripture] text means exposing Christ. If you're going to preach, then preach Christ,"[1] said J. Shaddix, the Chair of Expository Preaching at Southeastern Baptist Theological Seminary.

It's all about Jesus. God chose to pour all that he is and does into his Son. He gave the world and mankind to his Son, who redeemed it by his blood and gave it back to his Father. Everything else in our life and religion is secondary to the supremacy of this Jesus.

For this reason alone, I've chosen to publish Tom's works through EvangAlliance Publishing. In the millions of words he's written and preached, I cannot find anything other than Christ. No self-help, no prosperity, no self-indulgent pop-psychology, no emotional pandering—just Jesus.

Look for more books from Tom soon. Also, we will be bringing you movies telling, rather retelling, the greatest story ever told. And what is that story? It is the story of Jesus and how he uses ordinary people in extraordinary circumstances to reach those that are lost. Coming soon, you will find the remake of *The Cross & The Switchblade*, *Through Gates of Splendor*, *Run Baby Run*, and others.

May God bless you, and may the Jesus revealed in these pages—Immanuel—be precious to you.

Jim Palumbo,
PRESIDENT, EVANGALLIANCE PUBLICATIONS

---

1   J. Shaddix, *The Christ-Centered Expositor*, Tony Merida, B&H Academic, Nashville, TN, page 2